American Creative Writers on Class

Edited by Shelly Reed

American Creative Writers on Class
©2011, Big Wonderful Press

ISBN: 978-1-937806-00-2
LCCN: 2011942495

Authors Include: Michele Carlo; Oliver de la Paz; Caitlin Doyle; Monica A.Hand; Matthea Harvey; Sonya Huber; Emmy Hunter; Leslie Jamison; Rebecca Keith; Dorriane Laux; Laura McCullough; Colleen McKee; Christina Olson; Theresa Rodopoulos; and Carolyne Wright.   Editor and Introduction by: Shelly Reed

American Creative Writers on Class

Thank you to all the wonderful contributors and those
who were unable to contribute work, but offered
support, encouragement, and love.

Included in this Collection

Introduction by the Editor   9

Waitress   15
Dorianne Laux

Blue Teeth   17
Christina Olson

DiVida lives within her means   22
Monica A. Hand

Garbage Bag Wardrobe   23
Colleen McKee

7 oh 7   25
Michele Carlo

Spokane Reservation School Teacher:
Welpinit Washington   35
Carolyne Wright

In the Moment of Sun   37
Emmy Hunter

Paris   39
Caitlin Doyle

Brunetti Breaks it Down (or the Gospel
According to the 77th *Precinct*)   41
Rebecca Keith

Concerning the Strawberry, Concerning the
Navy Bean, and Jose the Liar   43
Oliver de la Paz

The Broken Heart of James Agee   50
Leslie Jamison

Minarets & Pinnacles   59
Matthea Harvey

The Fig and the WASP   60
Theresa Rodopoulos

Credit Rating, Butterfly Leisure,
and Reclamation   75
Laura McCullough

Waiting for the Placebo Effect   81
Sonya Huber

Contributors   95
Permissions & Acknowledgements   101

Introduction by the Editor

Why is it that layoffs, wage cutting, and union busting are called "business", but advocating for a minimum wage and universal health care is called "class warfare?" Are there not two sides? Of course there are, but the causalities are quite different. For the poor in America, there is a real danger of death or injury due to a lack of health care services, hunger, abuse, and poor working conditions . For the rich in America, the only real danger is being a little less rich. When both the consequences and the power are so heavily skewed, what can those of us with a moral interest do?

Unfortunately, there are many people who, after bettering their economic class (often with all the structure and assistance society can provide), choose to make it more difficult, rather than easier, for others to do the same. Psychological studies have shown that people are happy with their own economic success only if it is greater than that of their neighbors, not as it relates to their actual personal fortune. They want more comparatively, not more objectively, and sometimes it is easier to trip your neighbor in the race rather than run faster.

Our ultimate goal as humans should be to bring others up with us, not to hold them down. This requires a focus on education and opportunity, but it also means we need to reward actual work more and "letting your money work for you" less. Lately, we have heard the positive arguments for adopting universal health care and tax reform, but there is something we can do that we don't hear nearly enough: help each other.

I am not talking about charity, although that is good, I am talking about shopping at locally-owned stores instead of big chains, offering your employees benefits even when you don't have to, and leaving a decent size tip even if the waitress didn't smile enough for you. Get to know your neighbors and help each other.

By this time, you are groaning, "Of course I know that; of course I help my neighbors." You are reading this book, so maybe you do, but if you are anything like me, you need to be reminded all the time so you don't miss an opportunity. If we have to be reminded ourselves, than we must work twice as hard to influence those in our community who believe they owe nothing to anyone. Pay attention to the world, there are things you can do every day. Responsibility is contagious.

Most importantly, as we highlight in this collection, remember that while class does not indicate anything about a person's character, for good or ill, it does impact every part of our lives.

*****

This collection of work doesn't discuss necessary policy changes or force us to confront all the economic-based tragedies that occur in this country. Instead, we focus on intimate moments, personal relationships, and the common daily experiences shared at the intersection between people of varying economic class.

We start the book with Dorianne Laux's poem, *Waitress*. Like any miracle, it knocks us around a little and then shows us the light. No matter how difficult life can be, we all need to be reminded of the "grand phenomenon" of our breathing, conscious bodies.

Next, Christina Olson tackles the problem of the successful forgetting their start head on in her poem, *Blue Teeth*. It is even more difficult when you love the one who denies his/her roots. After all, there are very few among us who have never had a poor ancestor or an electricity cut-off notice.

Like Colleen McKee, many of us understand the challenges of that dreaded bag of donated clothing, that *Garbage Bag Wardrobe*. Like the child presented here, we don't need new things, but we certainly want them. Similarly, Monica A. Hand takes us inside the mind of her heroine, Diva, as she copes with life of economic insecurity in *Diva lives within her means*.

In *The Broken Heart of James Agee*, Leslie Jamison focuses our attention on the issue of class guilt to which none of us is immune. One often justified coping mechanism is that of turning our attention toward our own troubles, and sometimes, as was the case with James Agee, inventing them for this very purpose.

Oliver de la Paz blesses us with three poems of laborers, opening up both their reality, and humanity, in a way that feels like stepping into their skin. You will still see the berry stains on your hands for hours after reading *Concerning the Strawberry*.

Carolyne Wright's poem *Spokane Reservation School Teacher: Welpinit, Washington*, gives us a look into a nation inside a nation, another world, but one with the same class struggles. In *Brunetti Breaks it Down (or the Gospel According to the 77th Precinct)* by Rebecca Keith, we get a unique glimpse of class confrontation through the eyes of a crime victim during an interaction with the Bronx police.

While Catlin Doyle's interesting poem, *Paris*, shows us how much difference a generation of wealth can make in our view of the world, Emmy Hunter's poem, *In the Moment of Sun,* shows us a collision of people from many economic spectrums, all in real-time, or, as she puts it, "All this time has passed in the time of the poem."

In her three poems, Laura McCullough explores issues of class confrontation through the medium of a thrift store. Rejection of consumerism clashes with the embrace of it. But this comes through the embrace of a fairer kind of consumerism, a charity-inspired treasure hunt, one that brings with it the power of objects to initiate time travel, and the value of re-use.

Theresa Rodopoulos's *The Fig and the WASP* allows us have some fun while also touching on one of the most important elements to any ideological discussion on class – the psychological impact of economic vulnerability. If you have been there, you know that it impacts every part of your life. This is demonstrated perfectly in my favorite moment in the essay: "I had less to lose, but he was less convinced that loss was possible. Therefore, we reacted identically to risk, with equal measures of defiance."

In *7 Oh 7*, Michele Carlo gives us a story that makes us both angry and triumphant. You know those times that you wish you could have said that one perfect comeback, but never had the chance? Ms. Carlo did and she shares it with us.

We complete the collection with one of the most talked about aspects of the class issue in America, access to affordable healthcare. In *Waiting for the Placebo Effect* by Sonya Huber, we witness the personal experiences and fears of just one of the thousands of uninsured in America.

Enjoy the collection (and buy that bake sale cupcake),
Shelly Reed

Waitress
Dorianne Laux

When I was young and had to rise at 5 am
I did not look at the lamplight slicing
through the blinds and say: Once again
I have survived the night. I did not raise
my two hands to my face and whisper:
This is the miracle of my flesh. I walked
toward the cold water waiting to be released
and turned the tap so I could listen to it
thrash through the rusted pipes.
I cupped my palms and thought of nothing.

I dressed in my blue uniform and went to work.
I served the public, looked down on its
balding skulls, the knitted shawls draped
over its cancerous shoulders, and took its orders,
wrote up or easy or scrambled or poached
in the yellow pads' margins and stabbed it through
the tip of the fry cook's deadly planchette.

Those days I barely had a pulse. The manager
had vodka for breakfast, the busboys hid behind
the bleach boxes from the immigration cops,
and the head waitress took ten percent
of our tips and stuffed them in her pocket
with her cigarettes and lipstick. My feet
hurt. I balanced the meatloaf-laden trays.
Even the tips of my fingers ached.

I thought of nothing except sleep, a T.V. set's
flickering cathode gleam washing over me,
baptizing my greasy body in its watery light.
And money, slipping the tassel of my coin purse
aside, opening the silver clasp, staring deep
into that dark sacrificial abyss.

What can I say about that time, those years
I leaned against the rickety balcony on my break,
smoking my last saved butt?
It was sheer bad luck when I picked up
the glass coffee pot and spun around
to pour another cup. All I could think
as it shattered was how it was the same shape
and size as the customer's head. And this is why
I don't believe in accidents, the grainy dregs
running like sludge down his thin tie
and pin-stripe shirt like they were channels
riven for just this purpose.

It wasn't my fault. I know that. But what, really,
was the hurry? I dabbed at his belly with a napkin.
He didn't have a cut on him (physics) and only
his earlobe was burned. But my last day there
was first day I looked up as I walked, the trees
shimmering green lanterns under the Prussian blue
particulate sky, sun streaming between my fingers
as I waved at the bus, running, breathing hard, thinking:
This is the grand phenomenon of my body. This thirst
is mine. This is my one and only life.

16

BLUE TEETH
Christina Olson

In the photo of my father taken
        when he was twenty-five,
his front teeth, which he lost
        years earlier skateboarding drunk
into a tree, are cheap, noticeably blue.
        He didn't go to the dentist
often back then because he was afraid
        of needles, but now his teeth are nice
and he only notices bad teeth
        in others. Bad teeth are a sign
of poverty, of weakness.

        My father seems to have forgotten
all about the nights he slept
        in a VW bus on a queen mattress,
or the fact that his own father,
        son of Norwegian immigrants,
shared a bedroom with three siblings.
        My grandfather went to Michigan Tech
because he was too big an asshole
        to be a teacher. My great-grandmother
pulled him out of teacher's college
        after the first year and let him
be an engineer. Now, in our house,
        the gin is not cheap.
The Scotch costs even more.

My father would have been in the Army
        at the height of Vietnam, except
he won the genetic lottery

and got a medical discharge
for a bump on his scrotum
     that doesn't even hurt him.
At Thanksgiving, I try not to be
     a college-professor stereotype,
but it's difficult when my father says
     No, let's not go to that *McDonald's,*
it's gotten too black. In Buffalo,
     you can get really good Polish food,
but you will have to go to the neighborhoods
     where the Poles live, like Cheektowaga.
People from the north suburbs—me—
     call it *Cheektavegas* because
of the gaudy lights and plastic
     flamingos. Good *pierogies*, though.

Worse is the south side,
     which is where my father's second wife
grew up; now it's just block after block
     of rust and rubble, and if you don't lock
the doors of the Audi you're driving
     you *had that one coming. I grew up*
in Buffalo, I say to people
     who are not from Buffalo,
except when I have black students
     from Buffalo, and then I say
I grew up in Amherst. In 1998,
     Amherst was the safest community
in America. Then Dr. Slepian
     was shot at home in his kitchen,
bled to death in front of his wife
     and four sons, then a town in Colorado
called Littleton took our title.

Christina Olson

My father is big on *pulling yourself up
by your bootstraps*, which is fine with me
except what about the people
who don't have any boots?
To which my father says,
*If you're not a liberal at 20,
you have no heart, and if you're not
a conservative at 40, you have no brain,*
which is a clever line but not actually
Churchill's, it is from the nineteenth-century
Frenchman François Guizot.
Then my father shrugs
on his new leather jacket and warms
up the Audi. I know that he bought
the jacket at TJMaxx, because
that is how rich people get and stay rich,
and I know that he found the Audi
only after researching *Consumer Reports*

for six months, and all of this seems
more like something a formerly blue-toothed
man would do and not some jackass
just born rich. He and his new wife
winter on Longboat Key, which is between
working-class Bradenton and upscale Sarasota,
and once at a Sarasotan cocktail party
they mentioned Bradenton and the couple
they were talking to walked away
without another word. *Like I'd cut a fart!*
my father says, shaking his head at the memory.

My father's new vocabulary includes
      adjectives like *low-rent* and *section 8*,
and maybe he's earned them: he was sent
      off to college with just two suitcases,
no money. My father was a garbage man,
      drove a Tastee-Freez truck, learned
how to pour concrete. It took him ten years
      to finish his degree in geology. He did better
than his parents, but my generation will do
      about the same, if not slightly worse,
than our parents. My family is wealthy,
      but not rich. I will be comfortable,
but not wealthy, and damn lucky
      to have these straight teeth and my teenage
Amherst ennui. Meanwhile, some of my students
      are hard workers with limited skills,

and others are just hard workers,
      and some float along and take
education for granted. Those are the ones
      that keep me up at night. Still, I wish
my father would remember that it's pretty difficult
      to work hard in school and get into a good college,
a good state college, if you come from a family
      that is shattered and doesn't give a damn,
like some of my students' families,
      and that my students who stay up late
to study trigonometry are as rare as poets.
      I want those students to learn
to pull themselves up by their bootstraps,

but I also want this country to give them
some fucking boots to start with, or lessons
on how to wear boots, or to replace the straps for
free when they break, because contrary
to what my father might think, I know
my students will have to wait eight hours
in a hot and dirty waiting room with loud babies
and people yelling on cell phones
to even get those replacement bootstraps.
What I am saying is that we all have
blue teeth, even if they don't show
anymore when we smile. Look at
the family photographs, the really old ones
crumbling in the corners, look at the men
with their funny mustaches, look
into your great-great-great grandmother's
smile, *there*, there is the blue.

DiVida lives within her means
Monica A. Hand

Eats beans
Sleeps on the sofa
Home schools her progeny
Stuffs cardboard in her shoes
Washes her underwear in the sink
Grows tomatoes and cucumbers on windowsills
Spends her pension on travel to and from an alternative universe

The President's interrupts her favorite TV show with talk:

We will invest in medical research.
We will invest in clean energy.
We will invest in job training.
We will invest in education.

The rich don't need another tax cut –
                not if it means seniors can't eat

Sapphire mimics: million, billion, trillion –
                say it fast bet you choke on your own spit
I only got two dollars in my wallet
I can't afford the American dream

Pass the joint and put some ice in my Hennessy

Garbage Bag Wardrobe
Colleen McKee

"New clothes!" Mom would say. Big garbage bags of hand-me-downs from other moms in the trailer court. Or distant aunts from Arkansas. Or someone's boss, congratulating himself on his charity for giving us a sneak preview of his Goodwill pile. But mostly the bags came from other folks on food stamps.

The first couple of years, I was excited when I saw these bags, just because of the size of them. There had to be something good in there! My mom would pour the musty things out on my bed. I'd sort through them carefully, looking for new homes for my body. And sometimes there was something clean and soft inside, something with only the tiniest stain, something that almost fit. A shirt with an ironed-on star or Dyn-O-Mite! in curvy letters to stretch across my pudgy chest.

But by twelve I began to dread those bags. They were heaved from trailer to trailer, tied at the top with their own fraying plastic so that someone could save on twist ties. They'd rip open, white flags of surrender. Their cotton-poly guts would spill out. Those bags were full of roach spray, balls of lint, bruises. Yellow stains, dog hair, crusty cigarette burns. Everything worn by at least one or two kids, their longings and nightmares rubbed into the seams.

I was raised to know the difference between want and need. "You don't need new clothes," Mom would say. "You want them. You don't need them; you want them." I was raised inside a body that pinched at the seams.

7 Oh 7
Michele Carlo

When I was a child there was this animated commercial that ran on Spanish television.

As best I can recall, it went like this: It opens in a large kitchen, where a woman had just prepared a Thanksgiving dinner with all the trimmings. She carefully puts it all away then looks around with a contented sigh as she turns off the lights and, presumably, goes to bed.

In the dark, a lone cockroach scurries into view. It crawls up onto the counter and, upon seeing the coast is clear, it whistles and a host of cockroaches swarms in. They turn on the lights, make a pyramid to open the refrigerator door, carry out the turkey and other dishes, and embark upon a bacchanalia worthy of the golden calf worship scene in the movie *The Ten Commandments*—the one where Eddie G. Robinson's character Dathan cheers everyone on. Perhaps the roach leader did in fact sound like Eddie G. I wouldn't be surprised.

As the feast continues, the lady of the house is awakened from sleep. She runs to the kitchen in horror, and the roaches chase her out. She runs terrified back to her bedroom, picks up the phone and dials three numbers: 707. The instant she hangs up, a van screeches to a stop in front of the house, flings open its doors and an army of cans exit and dance (to a Latin beat) toward the house. The cans crash through the door and into the kitchen where, on sight, the roaches all freeze mid-bite and instantly drop dead. The closing scene has the lead 707 can shaking hands with the grateful lady while the rest march back to their van chanting, "Siete Zero Siete, matas cucarachas: 707 kills roaches."

Maybe Raid was more famous for "killing bugs dead" and Black Flag got a punk band named after it, but since I never saw that commercial on regular television, I'll bet only we Latinos had dancing insecticide cans. Funny thing is I don't remember the lady in the commercial being brown or beige...but blonde and pinky peach...

In the late 1920s and 1930s my grandparents had been what I call "Mayflower" Puerto Ricans, as they were among the first wave of islanders to arrive in New York City. As such, they were also part of the redefining of their neighborhoods: East (what later would be called Spanish) Harlem and the South Bronx. As an early 30-something in the early 1990s, I, too, was another pioneer of sorts, having already lived in pre-gentrification South Park Slope, Brooklyn, for five years, a neighborhood which then bore almost no resemblance to today's over-hyped/condo-bloated/latte-drinking/CSA-joining hipster Slope.

In the late 1980s, Prospect Park was not the carefully curated landscape it is today. It was a weed-choked frontier where homeless people showered in the Clorox-infused waterfall, and remnant debris from drug deals, anonymous trysts and various voodoo practices were strewn about the wooded areas. The now-acclaimed zoo was also far from its present incarnation as a "wildlife educational center." Instead, it was an unpatrolled warren of antiquated iron cages where, after closing, groups of misbehaving boys could easily sneak in. One late spring night, one of those boys climbed the wrong fence...and tragically became a bear's dinner.

And speaking of dinner, the two dueling Chinese take-out places on my block were rumored to serve "Blazer" and broccoli and "Snowball" in garlic sauce. Perhaps not the most-uncommon urban myth, but one that became eerily substantiated the day an Eyewitness News truck was seen in front of one of them. The restaurant closed that day, never to re-open. In fact, the storefront remained unrented for nearly twenty years afterwards, giving rise to another urban legend: that "Blazer" and "Snowball" had been haunting the place.

The neighborhood's line of demarcation was 9th Street, where the main Slope's stately Victorian brownstones slowly retreated into streets of red brick and limestone walkups. I had always lived above 9th Street, first above a definitely non-organic dry cleaner's, then in a rotting two-story building whose absentee landlord would not accept rent payments from tenants' hands, requesting instead they be taped to the apartment doors. Like many a 20-something before me, I endured the affordable squalor until one night, a rainstorm flooded the basement, or so we thought.

After a few weeks of calling the landlord to no avail, my new fiancé Adam and I braved the still ankle-deep waters and saw water gushing from the broken concrete floor and a sparking electrical cable hovering above. We immediately called the fire department, who said the building was in a state of imminent collapse and that all the tenants needed to move out fast! That is how I found myself in the back seat of a car service with a real estate broker I had called from a Village Voice listing.

Adam and I had thought we could "trade up" and move to the main Slope, but every apartment we saw was way beyond our budget. By late afternoon on the first day of our search, after having our hopes dashed several times, Adam had to go to work. I was then alone with the broker as the car went farther and farther up 7th Avenue. I had begun to despair of finding any apartment at all, and was about to say so, when the broker leaned toward me and said, "By the way, I wouldn't advise taking an apartment above 12th Street."

This not only seemed to come out of nowhere, it made no sense to me at all. The South Slope, for the most part, had long ceased to be, by any stretch of the imagination, a "'hood". If pressed to make any classification at all, I would have said the neighborhood was "religious," as every third block seemed to house a "Holy" something or other.

I asked, "Why?"

She leaned in closer and whispered, "Because that's where all the Puerto Ricans live."

Now she had no way of knowing that I had lived in that exact neighborhood for the past five years, because she hadn't asked and I hadn't volunteered. She also had no way of knowing what my ethnicity was, because she hadn't asked and, again, I hadn't volunteered. And why should I? I had spent much of my earlier life attempting to qualify and/or quantify what and who I was: the light-skinned, redheaded, freckle-faced "gringa" misfit of my Nuyorican family, or, the "spic" to many of the kids in the Italian and Irish neighborhood where I grew up.

Honestly, I was quite done with all of that. It was the 1990s. We were all supposed to be beyond petty racism and into multiculturalism, the gorgeous mosaic, and all that now ... right? Apparently not. Now I am not at all bilingual. My Spanish fluency, or lack thereof, had been the butt of family jokes my entire life, until the day I declared that I was proud to speak (mangle) the language like the American I was. But even my most critical Titi would have been proud of how I answered the broker:

"Claro? Seguro? La verdad? Los Puertorriqueños viven aqui? Me encanta los Puertorriqueños! Yo puedo comprar chuletas y alcapurrias, y..." Even though I was going through a (very short-lived) vegetarian phase, my subconscious desire for pork chops and meat pies was enough to make the real estate person's mouth hang open, albeit not from mouthwatering anticipation, as she said, "You...you...you're..."

As I looked at her quickly reddening face, I felt the same pit of shame in my stomach I had felt way too often while growing up. One of the reasons I defied my parents, and didn't want to live near them in the East Bronx when it was time for me to leave home, was that no way did I want to live among those who had bullied me for so long. Now that I was finally a full adult and presumably long-removed from all of that nonsense, here I was sitting next to yet another neighborhood purveyor of ignorance. Maybe I didn't have the presence of mind or vocabulary to counter this when I was growing up, but I did now.

"What?" I answered. "I can't be Puerto Rican? Why? Because I have red hair and freckles? I may be young, but I know what redlining is and you're doing it. I'm going to report you to the Better Business Bureau. Or better yet, I'm going to tell my father. He works at 100 Centre Street, you know, Manhattan Criminal Court."

I didn't tell her my father's job entailed screwing in the light bulbs there.

She turned from me and gave a different address to the driver than she had before. "I think this apartment might work for you," she said, without looking at me. I wasn't sure what had made her change her mind, but decided to wait and see. The car pulled down a side street to a grey stone house where an elderly couple sat on the porch. They greeted the broker warily, and I got the feeling there was, or had been, "something" between them. But the couple smiled at me and asked if I would like to see their top-floor apartment. I asked to use their phone and called Adam, begging him to come. I was so weirded out by the recent sequence of events that I didn't want to be alone. Luckily he managed to get an early break and soon arrived at the house. We looked at the upstairs apartment, which was kind of a wreck. The toilet leaked and there was no refrigerator in the kitchen, but since our present home was about to be condemned and this was the only place we had seen that was even close to our budget, we hoped they'd accept us.

The couple then invited us into their apartment and we all sat at the kitchen table. They told us they were originally from Sicily and their house had been in their family since

1905. I said that I had grown up in an Italian neighborhood and a lot of my friends had been Sicilian. This was the truth; I just left out that I wasn't also. My fiancé added that he had gone to St. Anthony's on MacDougal Street in Soho, which was also the truth. He just left out the part about being the only non-Catholic in the entire school. Yes, such a thing was possible, but that explanation is another whole story.

The couple first served us espresso, then biscotti, and finally homemade wine from the grapes growing in their backyard. They asked if we were married. We said, truthfully, "Not yet." They asked if we were both working. We said, truthfully, "Yes." They asked what our last names were and we told them: "Carlo and Gold." The couple then smiled at each other and said that "Yes, we could have the apartment," adding they were so happy to finally have a nice Italian girl and Irish boy move in because the real estate people had been sending them nothing but Puerto Ricans. Had I imagined there was an edge to the old woman's voice? I stole a look at the broker, but she sat stone-faced.

"Really?" I asked. "How could you tell they were Puerto Rican?" The man started to speak, but the woman cut him off to say that no one could put one over on her—no matter how white they might look she could always tell when someone was Puerto Rican. I got up to put my demitasse cup in the sink and stopped next to the woman, close enough to discern the faint aroma of baby powder with definite top notes of Ben Gay.

"Really?" I asked again. "How?"

"By their smell," she said.

The real estate broker jumped, no, sprang up and asked if she could speak with the couple privately for a moment. They went into the backyard and closed the door. Adam and I could hear voices, but couldn't tell whose they were. I looked around the kitchen and saw pots on the stove, a cutting board and vegetables on the counter. It looked as if she had been about to prepare dinner. When they all came back into the kitchen a moment later the elderly woman said, "You have a powerful friend here; not only are you getting a month's free rent, but also a new refrigerator and bathroom."

We signed the lease quickly, before anyone could change their mind.

Two weeks later, Adam and I invited our families to come to see our new apartment. I cooked my abuela's favorite dish, arroz negro con pulpo: black rice with octopus. It's very tasty but basically requires an apartment-wide fumigation after cooking. I've rarely cooked it again. I then turned the radio on to a salsa station—which I have never listened to before or since—and left the door ajar for sounds and smells to "waft" downstairs. As our new landlords opened their door to see what was going on, my family (including my café con no leche Aunt Carmen) and Adam's Litvak-featured family, coincidentally both arrived en masse. As everyone went up the stairs, the old couple looked from them to us in disbelief. I said, "Oh by the way, I'm Puerto Rican and my fiancé, he's Jewish!"

When the woman said, "Why didn't you tell us?"
I answered, "You didn't ask," and added, "Did I tell you my father works for Manhattan Criminal Court?"

The dinner was fabulous and our families went home secure in the knowledge that we were doing fine. But when my aunt got home she called and warned me not to leave any pocketbook, backpack or other bag on the floor until we got sprayed. It turned out she had brought a certain small, brown, six-legged stowaway home with her and had to buy something she hadn't needed in years—roach spray. We called the real estate broker who again convinced the landlord to pay for the spraying. I, for one, was glad that the truth was finally out and we all lived (mostly) at peace in that house for a very long time.

Sometimes, though, the irony of it all makes me laugh. Twenty years ago I was warned about the neighborhood being full of Puerto Ricans. These days, it almost seems like I'm the only one left.

Spokane Reservation School Teacher: Welpinit, Washington
Carolyne Wright

They used to have a dentist all day
Thursday. Now, you wait three months
or hitch to Spokane when the root's ache
breaks your stoicism down. Sharp operators
still cut Indians open at the B.I.A.
To live here, stay on automatic, keep
emergency systems on all night,
miss your lover only once a week.
When the bookmobile wheels in, hide there,
read how missionaries staked conversion
claims on tribes, worried at each others'
like tribe terriers over buffalo scraps.
Your school's an old God-trap of theirs,
earthed up now like a sod-sided council lodge.
Teenagers pass furtive peace pipes
through the fence at recess. If you weren't
the boss, brought from outside like a Jesus book,
you'd join them. Instead, you skirt the rules
like the obscene Salish scribbled
on latrine walls, follow the pretense
of coincidence, catch the braves red-handed.
Alright peace chiefs, back inside.
Finally Friday. You close the grade book
in the late light slanting over empty desks,
catch the last rush-hour rattletrap to town.
Your lover got the letter, thought it over,
lounges for you by the baggage counter.
All weekend you try to intersect
with something worth saying.

Carolyne Wright

Sunday evening, it's like your blood's run thin,
your language dying, buffalo gone north.
Nowhere left but the reservation.
The white man leaves you at the depot;
one quick kiss and he's gone, remote
as a black robe, council fires smoking
on far bluffs, a leaf spinning into the night.
Now you know how they felt.

In the Moment of Sun
Emmy Hunter

It comes in the beauty parlor,
A small concentration in the corner
Fumes and oranges,
A man requesting a wax,
A woman who immediately needs sequins.

This is what
I wanted to discuss.

Later, it happens again,
At Milk, on Poinsettia, near La Brea,
As I think of the cake with blue frosting,
All the delicious pleasures,
But left out

By Jews in small groups coming back

Without me,
What won't integrate, since this has no given
And I will have to shift everything or my meaning
If I am here.

The sun can come in through the shadow and tan you.

It's not always there. Other people may refuse to participate,
Like when I abruptly asked the man in the store
Where he'd gotten the *Times*.
But then someone spoke:
A tall woman needed to know
Why the dresses were forty dollars.

Let me return.
But it's ruined —
The "world of delicate human relations" in which
I tell that man to shut up.

But he wants to be quiet.

But what about
That woman?
The knife I used is still on her table,
A secret invader.

The haze surrounding the hills is tinged with
Medium-level particulates.
Every morning, her white car is covered.

The religious Jews
Have stopped coming.
It's no longer morning.

All this time has passed in the time of the poem.

The moment is the nail-salon women speaking Vietnamese.
It's important, an altar,
Close to the gas station and people with signs begging
In the lashing air.

Paris
Caitlin Doyle

"I don't want to be known as the granddaughter of the Hiltons. I want to be known as Paris."

Once you were a city.
    The young, hearing your name,
conjured cafes, the Venus de Milo,
    love along the banks. Now Paris
          is your face.
What changed so the Eiffel is your long-limbed
        height, the Seine your rivering hair?
Where did the Louvre go, leaving you in its place?

Not that you're not art,
    the angle of your head, your forward
hips. You pose in the lobby
   of the Texas Hilton, hot-pink mini skirt
      with luggage to match. We can hardly help
  ourselves, eye to belly-button
with your blank-canvas midriff
    on the magazine shelf.
But who pulled your skin so taut, who spread
    your easel-legs in that stance, no signature tells.
Unless you made your shape yourself.

Caitlin Doyle

Unless your shape
     was always there, implied in curving
staircases and long-stemmed
    champagne glasses, your father's
      father's father's fantasy; a bellboy dreaming
his own hotel. If you saw him now,
     you wouldn't see him,
any more than armless Venus, if she met her creator,
could embrace him. The bellboy carries your bags for you,
     watching through the elevator door
     as you step from view.

Brunetti Breaks it Down
(or the Gospel According to the 77th Precinct)
Rebecca Keith

So, did you notice any guys in the park? Can you describe
the guys in the park? It was probably one of the guys in the
park. Don't go to the pawnshops past Franklin by yourself.
Don't go past Franklin at all. Over there the crime is drug-
related. Over here, they come here to rob you. Over there,
the perps usually know the victims. Over here, they're on
your fire escape. You can try the pawnshops, but I don't think
you'll recover anything. I don't recommend going by yourself.
There was a second guy? This guy was crazy. This guy
wouldn't give a name. Had no ID. Had a USB cable in his
pocket. Said, *Matthew, Matthew, I'm not running.* Looked up
towards the roof. They checked the roof—*Clear!* Oh, you
must mean my partner. I'm the good looking one. He's the
other one. *Clear!* We get a lot of people trying to give us
drawings of the stuff they lost. Not bad. This guy was sitting
on your bed. This guy left fingerprints all over your desk. No,
those are yours. This guy dumped all your jewelry out in a
tangled mess on the bed. Didn't find the tiny sapphires, only
valuable piece you own. Threw all the laptops in a
pillowcase. His fingers on your pillow. Looked at the picture
of you and your boyfriend on your desk. Looked at your bras
hanging to dry. Looked at your piles of magazines. Maybe ate
a cracker from the box you left out. Maybe washed his hands
in the tempered glass bowl sink. That sink: why the
apartment looks like a condo but is really a rental with
slipshod construction. This guy was it one guy or two guys?
Didn't take the TV. Didn't take the guitar. Didn't take the

camera. The checkbooks. The passport. They were junkies.
Crackheads. They were not the lady who wheels the cart
with the cans and the skeletal lamp frame. Down to the Met
Food, back to the park. Wears her down coat in the summer.
Keeps her head covered. Always with the lamp. They came in
through the empty lot. Hopped the fence. Squeezed through
the gate. Reached up for the ladder. Entered through the
emergency exit. Non-escape through the fire escape. It must
have been one of the guys in the park. They're always in the
park. Have you noticed anything different? Have you noticed
the park? Look, the snow is melting. You can see the Wash-
n-Lube sign neon from your window but soon you'll see
green. Those six to eight trees almost make you forget
Atlantic and its squall of traffic, bumpers and glass spun out
in the intersection— skid, honk, exhaust. The view from your
roof, where the second guy was, if you take away the yellow
Brothers Storage building, look the other way— south, west,
even a little east— church spires and gardens, warm-lit
windows. See, you could hop someone else's fence, pull
down their ladder, heave yourself up through their window
and take your place.

Concerning the Strawberry
Oliver de la Paz

I've told you everything about the fields
except one thing, and it is something

I had spared you from because it is a hard thing
to hear. In June, there are strawberries—

strawberries and the fingers of workers
reddened by bruised fruit. And when the hands

get a hold of this color, sticky and sweet
with a metallic smell, they wipe them

on their pants. Sometimes
their thighs stiffen from the juice

and sometimes fruit flies swarm
these men, their bodies a slow-walking feast.

Of course, June is a hot month
and when their skin touches the cotton

of their clothing, the heat makes
a syrup they carry home after many hours

bending and plucking. And when they are home
with the few garments they own, the men wash

in a wooden basin, the clothes that had soaked
the field into each fiber. It is the color

that is the hard part. It doesn't come off
no matter how long and hard the men scrub

with pumice stones and soap. They rub
the stones into cloth so long

the skins of their hands peel back
making even more red. Listen,

the months are long and the strawberry
stays with you. It will cover your bed

and it will speckle your dreams. Listen,
friend, for it will hold you

in its sweet liquor, its savage heart
plump and thrumming.

Concerning the Navy Bean
Oliver de la Paz

At evening over a low fire, we roast
a can of beans, and listen to the gurgle
and pop as water comes to a boil.

It's beans for dinner and nothing else,
while Jose fathoms an impossible meal:
steak or salmon, something savory

to eat with a fork and a bib.
I tell him to keep his prayers
on common-sense things, like gloves

without holes, or boots to stand all day in,
some long pants, a wide brimmed hat.
But beans are not these—

little balls of gas, little dicots turning
in their stew, they smile and bob,
toiling as water turns to steam.

The flames of our oaths light up the sky
like pistol shots in the dark,
reckless with our hunger-anthems

which keep us warmer than a can of beans
over a flame. Everywhere
the pyrotechnics of dinner sizzle—

a thing hums deep within our skulls
while our hands and backs remember
rows of corn or lettuce or peas, the stem

tugs as the last of the bounty
plunks into our buckets, then
on to a truck for Fresno or somewhere

where there's white wine on ice,
broiled pheasant garnished
with crisp apples, the god of the table

somewhere off stage. Our galaxy
could do without beans tonight,
and the stars forget the small fires

all over the valley made by men with similar loves.
We are hungry and without
hats or gloves . . . without the luxury of

answerable prayers, or the perspective of stars.
And now over our fire, a bit of juice
from the can jumps into the pit

marking time with a hiss. We count out
equal portions, dividing beans
between us to celebrate work

at the end of the day when it's all over
with nothing in our hands except spoons
we raise to the shift bosses and to trucks

Oliver de la Paz

heading to Fresno and to this land,
vast and dark in the night time
and to the brother at the end of the row

and Jose will tell us
beautiful lies about the white houses
over the hill and he'll do this

with a mouthful of beans—
beans

47

Jose the Liar
Oliver de la Paz

We were half baked in the filaments of light bulbs
and conveyors spitting cans past our hands
when Jose said the most bald-faced bull I've ever heard

starting with him taking the McGregor girl out
for a spin in borrowed jalopy with a bottle
filled with mash, three-parts alcohol to one-part

diesel, and he took this girl and this whiskey
and drove past the shift boss's house, past the railroad
where the vagabonds wait for the jump to Modesto,

past all those bunkhouses along the farms near the back end
of town, where the old church judges all, and he took this girl
up the canyon to the bluff overlooking the city

and Jose leaned in real close to tell me while the cylinders
sped by, the McGregor girl smelled like sampaguitas,
that her eyes could break men's knees the way a mallet

strikes a spike, that she was "familiar" with men, whiskey
and other worldly things, and I wanted it to be
true as the clank of the tin cans in the factory, as the noise

cracking through our ears was real, and I wanted
the McGregor girl to be all freckle and bone
like my hands, reddened by the speed of work—I wanted

to believe that a few hours could be spent
driving nowhere with a girl and a bottle, and how some roads
open into vistas and some roads lead the hell out of here,

that you could see the half-mile over the shacks in the valley,
standing next to a beauty who's crazy about you or maybe
crazy about your danger, and that you could crack a smile or

laugh at youth and the shift boss's stupid dog
somewhere above the ball-bearing noise on a road,
dusty, the color of wheat, as far away as truth.

The Broken Heart of James Agee
Leslie Jamison

Many nights that autumn we went to a bar where the floor was covered with peanut shells, and we drank ourselves silly, and I talked about James Agee. I'd drink two vodka tonics before Sam showed up and read Agee while I drank them. I let myself get weepy at the horror of what he wrote. Liquor carried the trauma all through me, twisted me pliable to the loss, and then Sam came, and we switched to cheap wine, and I explained to him what I'd taken into my heart. I wasn't afraid to speak like this, *taken into my heart*, because I was drunk. Drunk meant sentiment was not only permissible but imperative. It was boundless.

Turns out *Let Us Now Praise Famous Men*[1] wasn't about famous men. I had a lot to say about this, and other things as well. I had a lot to say about how Agee had wanted to fuck one of the poor women he wrote about, and how he was willing to confess it, and I had a lot to say about bedbugs and denim overalls and farmhouses like cracked nipples on the land. I had a lot to say about how Agee had a lot to say about guilt.

Turns out *Let Us Now Praise Famous Men* was a magazine article gone rogue. In 1936, *Fortune* told Agee to write an article about sharecroppers in Alabama, and he gave them a spiritual dark night of the soul instead. They promptly rejected it. So he wrote another 415 pages. He

---

[1] Agee, James. *Let Us Now Praise Famous Men*. Photographs by Walker Evans. Boston: Houghton Mifflin, 1941.

couldn't think of another way to speak what he'd found. It's a hard book to classify: it's got sections that don't seem to belong together: discussions of food and clothing and salary and the soul as an angel nailed to a cross: it uses colons somewhat like this sentence does, rabidly. It's an angry book, both proud and ashamed of its attempt to do something ethically necessary, which is to describe the material and spiritual condition of American poverty. It's so long-winded and beautiful you want to shake it by the bones of its gorgeous shoulders and make it stop. It doesn't stop. The impossibility of closure is one of its obsessions: the endlessness of labor, hunger, and desire. "The plainness and iterativeness of work," Agee writes, "must be one of the things that makes it extraordinarily difficult to write of." It just goes on and on.

This notion struck me deeply: the possibility of a story made difficult to tell by the same traits, the damage of drudgery and monotony, that made it worth telling in the first place. I'd always been a teller of stories. I'd always earned my place at the table by way of narrative: anecdotes at cocktail parties (*Behold these priceless ironies! The curiosity cabinet of my past!*) and intricate dissections of childhood wounds, essays that proved I could shape my life into something worth hearing about. Now Agee was saying: there are lives you can't possibly compress into narrative.

I was trying, at that point in my life, to figure out how to tell a story of my own. I'd recently returned to America after a brief stint in Nicaragua, in a town called Granada, where I'd been mugged and punched in the street late one night, drunk. My nose had been broken and then partly fixed by an expensive surgeon in Los Angeles. I'd been teaching second-graders in Granada, but back in those early days the kids were largely lost to me—when I thought of Nicaragua, I thought mainly of my own face.

I'd moved to New Haven, where it seemed like someone was always getting mugged, and I was afraid to walk alone in the dark. I liked walking home with Sam, when we were drunk, and there was snow, and a moon—and we could forget about Agee and his sharecroppers and everyone on the streets of New Haven, and we could go home, go to bed, surrender to the privacy of sex or blackout sleep or both, in quick succession.

"Nearly all is cruelly stained," Agee wrote, "in the tensions of physical need." There's a notion we can absorb, about suffering, that it should somehow expand us or render us porous, but this didn't happen to me. I felt shrunk. *In the tensions of physical need.* Damage becomes need, almost immediately. It becomes an insistence. I read Agee writing about himself, his own guilt, when he was supposed to be writing about three Alabama families, and I found myself thinking about myself when I was supposed to be thinking about Agee.

Or else, I thought of everyone who wasn't me, on the streets of Granada. I thought of the boys I'd tutored some afternoons—most of them homeless, many addicted to glue—with leftover worksheets from school, catching them as they prowled the cantinas of Calle Calzada, looking for money and company. I thought of Luis, who'd fallen asleep on the steps of the group home where I lived—and how I hadn't invited him inside, only woken him up, nudged his shoulder, because he was blocking the door. I inspected the memory for the shown seams of a moral: what should I have done? I inspected the mirror to find the crooked bone on my face.

I loved getting drunk and getting sad about Agee because his sadness was *other* to mine; it did not feel tainted by self-concern in the same way my own did. There was so much claustrophobia in my guilt, my memory, my face. But Agee was somewhere else. He was another thing. He was a thing I wasn't. He delivered me into the terrible song of what he'd found. *Tragedy is second-hand.* Faulkner wrote that. He put it in the mouth of a rich man lost to drink. Families in Alabama hurt more than I ever would, and I could show up at a dingy bar and admit this to myself, could confess it. This was not enough, but it was something. Agee felt this about his own book: it was not enough but it was something. He writes of a woman's endless daily work on cotton fields:

> "how is it possible to be made clear enough...the many processes of wearying effort which make the shape of each one of her living days; how is it to be calculated, the number of times she has done these things, the number of times she is still to do them; how conceivably in words is it to be given as it is in actuality, the accumulated weight of these actions upon her; and what this cumulation has made of her body; and what it has made of her mind and of her heart and of her being."

Empathy is contagion. Agee catches it and passes it to me—to all of us. He wants his words to stay in everyone as "deepest and most iron anguish and guilt." They have stayed; they do stay—they catch as splinters, still, in the open palms of this essay.

How do you talk about how other people hurt? Agee doesn't answer. He only wonders what it might look like— an adequate description, *what this cumulation has made*—and suspends that possibility in the margins of his book: everything he can't manage.

If he'd had his way, he wouldn't have written a book in the first place. "If I could do it, I'd do no writing at all here," he says. In this way, we are prepared for the four hundred pages of writing that follow.

> "It would be photographs," he continues, "the rest would be fragments of cloth, bits of cotton, lumps of earth, records of speech, pieces of wood and iron, phials of odors, plates of food and of excrement. Booksellers would consider it quite a novelty; critics would murmur, yes, but is it art; and I could trust a majority of you to use it as you would a parlor game."

> "A piece of the body torn out by the roots might be more to the point"

In the third grade, we spent a week building Native American villages from mud. On the last day, Ms. Cohen marched across the lawn in her heavy black boots and trampled each village back to dirt. I tell this story now and people laugh at liberal pedagogy, how it offers nine-year-olds handfuls of clay and picture books of sweat lodges and bearable doses of betrayal—but I still remember what I felt that day: glad I hadn't been one of those people, with their villages wrecked, and angry at Ms. Cohen for making me participate in their loss.

On the question of what poverty does to consciousness, Agee is merciless—and, for once, succinct: "the brain is quietly drawn and quartered". His book does the same to its story, slicing it to pieces and putting it back together in fragments strung together by the ubiquitous colon: the house, the dawn, the animals, the men, Communism, textbooks, children. He calls his work, "the effort to perceive simply the cruel radiance of what is."

What is, it seems, was broken. So Agee broke his book to fit. Subject holds structure in its thrall. Poverty pulls apart identity instead of fusing it into anything whole; Agee pulls apart narrative rather than rendering it coherent. *Drawn and quartered.* Agee doesn't think he'll ever do justice to the families he writes about: "I feel sure in advance that any efforts, in what follows, along the lines I have been speaking of, will be failures." Agee chokes on his words, commas and clauses, interrupting to say nothing. He stutters here. He stutters often.

Back in the states, with a cast on my face, I took a map of Granada and tried to make it my own. I carefully marked important spots and wrote an accompanying legend: *Where I lived first; where I lived second; where we drank the best rum, where we drank the worst rum, where we danced to Shakira, where the woman sold mangoes for cheapest, where I was hit.* Where I was hit. As if I could.

As if I. I stutter too. I stutter when I try to say it, still—*I was hit on the face in the street*—and feel ashamed, at my stuttering, such an overreaction. I hear the voice of someone I have never met, saying this to me, and cannot disagree with them.

But in those early days, I thought I could put my hit on a map, make it a landmark, transfigure it easily into a joke no one was around to hear. What was Agee's word? A novelty. I thought I'd make a parlor game of cloth and clods of earth, puffs of cotton and plates of shit. I was joking because I felt the world was asking me not to take it personally, the hit, and I took it personally. I kept trying to make it something larger than itself, that fucking *single moment*, to make it part of a map or a pattern.

The easiest pattern was guilt. My hand had been on a sleeping boy's shoulder, shaking him awake. What does concrete make you dream? I dream of him in circles. I could think forever about the man that hit me, round and round—how little he had, most likely, and how big a difference it might have made to him, to sell my little digital camera wherever he sold my little digital camera—that camera I would have given him easily, just to keep him from hitting my face.

I went somewhere to look at poverty, and I left damaged. Agee went somewhere to look at poverty, and he wanted to take the damage onto himself, to make it felt, to strip away its metaphors and get to some clean, hard, torn truth beneath—"the literal feeling by which the words a broken heart are no longer poetic, but are merely the most accurate possible description."

What was broken in me was not poetry. It wasn't useful as metaphor or aperture.   My face was only the accurate description of where a hand had been. *My hand had been.* The dream keeps to its circle.

It doesn't seem right to say Agee risked sentimentality. Or verged into it. Better to say: he embraced it. He could smell it from a mile off and he clawed his way into it anyway. He fought it except when he fought for it. He thrust it before him like an obscenity, forcing everyone to see what outrage had driven him to the embarrassment of such hyperbole. One feels, often, infected by it.

William Vollman, bad-boy bard of degradation, considers himself one of Agee's descendants. He describes *Praise* as a battle between ferocious intellect and sentimental naiveté:

> "despite its fierce intellectualism it is essentially an outcry of childlike love, the love which impels a child to embrace a stranger's legs...his heart went out to them, and he fought with all his crafty, hopelessly unrequitable passion to make our hearts do the same...repeatedly falls on its sword."[2]

I spent my first two years of graduate school writing essays about Agee. What good is guilt? Sometimes it makes us act. Sometimes it doesn't. Sometimes it makes us talk about ourselves—our own experience of someone else's suffering—for pages and pages, because we are

---

[2] Vollmann, William. *Poor People.* New York: Ecco, 2007.

trying to purge something even our confession won't justify. That dreaming boy. You get drunk—and then you get sentimental, or else you get hit.

What good is guilt? We like the sound of the question. It puts a crude finger on a heartbeat in us that won't stop racing, a pulse broken in sympathy. We never stop asking.

Agee drank when he wrote, and I drank when I read him. Agee threw himself at the feet of his subjects, and I couldn't even bring myself to walk alone at night, with my bone-broken nose and my wine-flung and fluttering heart. I told myself there was something dense and meaningful in my fear—an earned experience, the residue of contact, a cruel radiance—but truly there was nothing but my arms crossed over my chest, as I walked on dirty streets, and no one coming after me in the dark.

MINARETS & PINNACLES
Matthea Harvey

Around 5 o'clock even the grounded crowds of ageing coquettes
who still believed the bat of an eyelash or two could cause the miracle

of upward mobility, stood still, watching the tangerine streaks of sunset.
They did not remember why they did it. Ties to God had proven fickle —

first the prayermats were put in the pantry in case the maid happened to upset
the olive oil & then the gold podiums seemed perfect for those lengthy articles

about real estate & roof repairs. At night, tucked in their towers, they dreamt
of falling, as most people do, but though they'd been told the tale of Babel,

their situation was admittedly different: this was each man & his minaret.
Capitalism on the up and up. Pinnacles of success moved from the hypothetical

to the real: now you picked your peak & started climbing. Naturally it was getting
harder & harder to find an available & presentable mosque — smaller conical

structures called Mini-Minarets were being very successfully marketed.
Members of the upper class, cramped on their sagging balconies, cast cynical

smiles at their new neighbors. They liked to languidly take out their lorgnettes
& study the wet patches under the upstarts' armpits & their awful freckles

while feasting on roast duck hoisted up just that morning, sipping anisette,
& making sure to ignore what was going on below: some troublesome radical

who looked a bit like a ballerina was letting her toes touch the ground, pirouetting
around that dark and dirty square as if she loved it — which was truly inexplicable.

The Fig and the WASP
Theresa Rodopoulos

We met at private college. I was there on full financial aid
because my family made squat. He was there because his
boarding school had an Ivy League pipeline.

The Druzhba pipeline is the longest oil pipeline in the
world. It was built in the 1960s and leaks something
awful. Black lakes of oil all across central Russia.
"Russians can't take care of business," said Uncle Vito.
Uncle Vito poured cement in Queens. My uncles built that
borough. "Fuck the grid," said Uncle Vito. "The grid is for
those Manhattan mother-fuckers." The way to drive
through Queens: kiss your fingertips, shut your eyes.
Driving in Queens is Italian duende.

Duende, wrote Lorca, "is not a matter of ability, but of real
live form; of blood; of ancient culture; of creative action."

"Another thing," said Uncle Vito. "Have you ever noticed,
good Jews are Jews but bad Jews are Russians?"

My parents have three ex-spouses between them. Two
Jews, one Russian. In first grade, my mother told her
Jewish teacher that she was Jewish, too. The teacher
called Yiayia and Yiayia dislocated my mother's arm. Now
my mother's right arm is longer than her left arm, but she
can still recite the pistevo.

In the war, I don't know what war, probably an undeclared war, a mountain-people war, where her Yiayia's Yiayia came from, partisans arrived in the villages and told the children to genuflect. In heaven, a cross is a cross, but on Earth, where we were put to suffer, the devil is in the details. Up-down-left-right, they lived. Up-down-right-left, they died.

My mother didn't know how to say "Where's the bathroom?" in Greek, so the Orthodox priests let her wiggle until she peed in her tights. At St. Lucy's, East Harlem, the Mother Superior was a mean six-footer and beat my father with a rubber hose. He played hooky across the footbridge on Randall's Island while a young black man on a Dray horse with a pistol in his belt rode in circles keeping order. Every day: a can fight or a seizing epileptic. Back then you jammed a bat handle between the jaws, but now you flip the person over, let them contemplate the ground.

Growing up white, wealthy, and rural in the 1950s, his parents were interpolated rather gently. They were impeccably educated and industrious. They spent their whole lives earning—in retroaction—the undemonstratively enjoyed privilege that was their birthright. Cabled sweaters in the wintertime. In the summer, tennis on the Cape.

Of course, they had dreck in the duende department.

In the house where he grew up, no one ever shouted. No
one ever said, "I love you." When he hugged his father,
they angled their bodies a little bit to the side so their
dicks didn't touch.

Really he'd have rather his dick disappeared. Dicks are
like crowbars, crude tools to get you inside. He was born
an insider. He wanted to pretend he didn't know how he
got there.

His name was Harlan, but not for any particular reason. I
am named for my father's mother and my father is named
for his mother's father and my mother is named for her
mother's mother and my brother is named for our
mother's father. I've counted; there are only eleven
names in my entire family, the Greek side and the Italian
side put together. My father has a daughter from his first
marriage. She's named for his mother, too. If we ever
meet it will be awkward for many reasons.

Every year, his parents took in a gifted student from the
Caucus Mountains or the Asian Steppes. His mother's
favorite— Bernadette—came from Lithuania. I saw
pictures from her wedding, bride and groom outside the
red brick church in Vilnius. All the men in Vilnius: tall, dark
Prince Charmings. The women delicate and fair in pale
blue dresses like spun glass.

My gender dysphoria didn't register with my father. I called him from my dorm room on my roommate's cordless phone. I said, "Pop, I'm going to cut my hair like James Dean." It was seven am. He needed to catch the

Ave A bus uptown to light the ovens at Empire Pizza and sounded pissed. "You wanna look like a fucking Protestant?"

Harlan's mother told me Druzhba means "friendship."

Years later, when he failed to pursue an advanced degree or follow some other path towards professional specialization, he attributed his dissolute lifestyle—which included drug abuse, kleptomania, and veganism—to punk music. Long past the golden years of his adolescence, he harbored a lingering, peevish commitment to certain analytically underdeveloped anti-authoritarian principals, which he couldn't specify. But they existed. Otherwise, he would have had a hot girlfriend, a gym membership, and maybe a successful architecture firm.

For him, failure was, ipso facto, a transgression. As a revolutionary model, I found this somewhat lacking. I wanted to build a robust alternative counter-public, an outwardly focused community in creative process. I wanted expanded kinship networks, a new poetics for living and dying, a kind of perpetual fluxing, an animate architecture, something ardent, something ownerless and open.

Once my father met some hippies from a commune out in New Mexico. They gleaned road kill from the freeways and made huge stews for communal meals. "I heard later those hippies got the plague and died," said my father. "That what you're talking about?"

Harlan's cornflower eyes made his silence seem affable, so it was easy to fill in his side of the conversation. He was a big white screen onto which I projected image after image. I wanted to be loved by Descartes. I wanted to be scissored between the golden axes of modernity, cut into a paper doll of myself, pretty and uncomplicated.

He was like the Enlightenment. He was like a right angle. A room with no shadows. Clean and straight and clear. I was a bramble, a clod of dirt, weeds, overgrowth too dense for the sun to penetrate, dark wedges, or festers.

At twelve, he had a paper route in Gladwyne, PA, but felt so uncomfortable collecting money that he ended up paying for the whole town's subscriptions out of his birthday bank account. At twenty-five, he was a huge tipper—30% every time. I loved his largesse. He liked to squander himself: his money, his talent, his intelligence. He opened a tab and forgot his credit card at every bar we ever went to.

I thought he seemed Danish, in this very well-built way. A tall, princely Dane: naturally athletic, with a round face and soft features and feathery blonde hair. He had never broken a bone. No one he knew personally had ever died. His neck was columnar. I made plans to climb up his neck and stand on top of his head. I wanted to stay up there for 37 years, like a new Simon Stylites. I was too nervous to pursue intimacy through the usual channels.

Actually, he was a little faggy. Most straight people didn't notice, but queers did. Hetero-normativity filled me with terror so I gave him the benefit of the doubt.

In her prime, Yiayia took a lot of men for not too much money. According to Yiayia, it is much better to take one man for a lot of money. "Unless you like variety," said Yiayia. She didn't. "If you get a box of shit shaped like chocolates," said Yiayia. "It doesn't matter if you pick a truffle or a cherry cream."

Everyone in the family talks about how beautiful Yiayia was—her green eyes and black hair, how she was the only Patricopolous in history with tits—but by the time I came around she was a fat, bewigged Greek grandma in a tent dress with lipstick-stained teeth.

Exactly like all the others.

She knew enough not to wear gold lamé before five.

In 1822, a German mineralogist developed a method for comparing the scratch resistance of different minerals. Diamond got a perfect ten. Tiffany's! Cartier! Black Starr! Frost Gorham! In Yiayia's day, the girls tested their engagement rings on shop windows. They cut heart-shaped holes in the glass ceiling and wiggled through with much damage to their shoulder pads.

Auntie Eleni: You're a very smart girl.

Auntie Gigi: Very smart.

Auntie Eleni: Too smart to work so hard.

Yiayia: Why do you want this, this B.A.? It's like hitching yourself to a wagon.

Auntie Eleni: Better off with a M.R.S.

Auntie Gigi: That's right, a M.R.S.

Yiayia: Those letters go before your name.

When midterms came around, neither of us studied. I squeezed grapefruit juice into mason jars and we sipped Everclear Greyhounds on the bridge over the polluted canal. The canal stank and I was sure it wasn't more than ankle deep. He thought it was six, maybe eight feet deep. "Let's jump," he said, and we were both straddling the short fence when the bicycle cops blew their whistles and sent us home. For years I thought this proved that we were willing to die for each other.

I had less to lose but he was less convinced that loss was possible. Therefore, we reacted identically to risk, with equal measures of defiance.

We drove the rental car into Arkansas for a handle of Old Crow. We drank half of it and broke the bottle on the pavement. Scene beneath the streetlight. Scene on the king-sized bed. He wielded the broken bottle like a feather duster, jagged glass just brushing my breast, fine white lines scratched in dry skin, not even pink. "Cut me," I said. But he couldn't so I put my hand on his hand and I twisted and I was cut and bled hard. In the morning, we admired the musky spatter—blood and bourbon—but felt guilty about the housekeepers. We balled up the sheets and took them with us.

I didn't believe in reified object choice. I believed in fields of desire. At the same time, I wanted him bound to me at the cellular level. I was raised on Eucharist and fascism. I didn't want a boyfriend so I made him my blood brother. "We are warrior-lovers," I said, and he didn't say anything, which was as much an assent as I needed.

Post-college he had no plans. I went home to Yiayia's apartment, wrote him emails from the library on Houston

Street, propositions for expatriation, blue prints for our triumphant adulthood:

I am contemplating a move to the severe coast of Wales.
I have been considering the Romanian forest— torches,
staves, one meal a day of sour black bread and
gooseberry jam. We can scuttle around the clock, fulltime
scuttling, scuttling in mantels to the riverbank, scuttling to
the cauldron to stir bitter greens. We can become crones,
battle with badgers/hawks/wolves, weather unspeakable
winters. You can be wattle and I can be daub. It will be
grim and desperate and the woods will be peopled with
Germanic water spirits and demons.

What about goats in the Peloponnesus? I have some
wretched family in a little mountain town: white houses
balanced on rocks, figs and cyclamen, narrow shade of
the cypress. The widows will bring us honey and coffee
while we hang cheeses in the cool ruins of the tiny
churches. Or we can move to the islands. Or to
Campagna.   I have ten thousand cousins in the vineyards
south of Naples. You can see the mouth of Vesuvius glow
in the night. The beds are just rushes and boards. The
wine is from the cellar. Or we can move to Chicago.
There are flea markets and vegan Korean food. We can
live in Bangkok Royal Garden. In an air-stream trailer. In
a tree-house. In a sand-dune. In an amphitheater in a
blighted urban park. I know just the one. Inside, it has a
graffiti skull and red cursive that reads, "blood is what
makes us real."

On average, women say 7, 000 words a day and men, 2, 000.

Harlan's trust fund will kick in the same year the Mayan calendar kicks out.

Yiayia kept a man's belt in the house. My mother scraped her forearms on the bricks so when she got upstairs she was already bleeding. Yiayia, reduced to a half-hearted backhand.

In 1960, Yiayia got a man killed. She fenced him the gold bullion that her brother Jimmy stole from the airport. The man who got killed was a Jewish jeweler, a family man with a little store on West End Avenue. He thought Yiayia was sexy and Sephardic. He got shot in the heart and died right where they built Lincoln Center.

Yiayia was not my father's mother. Yiayia was my mother's mother. So far none of the girls have been named for her, which makes it my job to have a daughter. My daughter will be called Kanella: Greek for cinnamon. It's also the Spanish word for cinnamon; Spanish, like all the world's languages, is a degraded form of Greek.

After a semester studying theory, I came home for Christmas Eve. Seven fishes on the table and I didn't eat one bite. "I'm a vegetarian," I said. "Also, this possessive investment in Greek and Italian ethnic identity—it's white supremacist. It has to stop. We need to examine the social and economic mechanisms of racial formation."

Yiayia said, "I know, princess. The other day I was so embarrassed. I was out with cousin Joannie and a man in the park thought she was Puerto Rican."

During a history seminar, Harlan read about his maternal grandfather, Robert Wilder, in a book about Martin Luther King. That night, we rode bikes to the river and drank Narragansett tallboys, back to back on the packed ground, dampness coming up through our Dickies, crumpled cans in the bushes, and shredded plastic bags.

The Montgomery Advertiser, November 14, 1956:

Laws requiring racial segregation on buses in Montgomery and throughout Alabama were declared unconstitutional yesterday in another historic decision by the U. S. Supreme Court. But from white leaders of the city and state came warnings of possible violence and bloodshed if any attempt is made to carry out the decision. Robert Wilder, local leader of the pro-segregation Montgomery Citizens' Council chapter, predicted flatly that "any attempt to enforce this decision will inevitably lead to riot and bloodshed."

Jean Toomer moved to the town where Harlan grew up in the 1940s and died the same year Robert's oldest grandson was born. In boarding school, Harlan read *To Kill a Mockingbird* and also *Cane*. He thought both books were very affecting.

His parents met on a warm spring night, some sock hop or semi-formal, a mixer for the Haverford boys and the girls of Bryn Mawr. James played sweeper on the varsity soccer team and Albertine had just returned from Paris. At the boarding house, the girls—American, French, Italian, and Spanish—communicated with one another in Virgil.

James thought Albertine's southern accent was simply darling. Data fata secutus.

My parents met at a rent strike in Brooklyn. They lived in the same slum on Ocean Avenue. Their downstairs neighbor, Valerie, put a bowl of chicken blood outside her door and that week, in a Park Slope restaurant, the landlord slipped on a disc of battered eggplant and broke his leg.

Drunk on Carlo-cola (a family favorite: jug wine and coke), my mother explained again how she was going to shove a knitting needle through the bastard's eye and kill him in his sleep. She had the needle on the table, metal, double pointed. I'd never seen her knitting anything. The bastard was my father, smoking his cigar by the window, unconcerned.

Auntie Eleni: Penelope was blind in one eye.

Yiayia: She never slept.

Auntie Gigi: If there was company, she slept.

Auntie Eleni: She went into her bedroom, maybe, with the light off.

Yiayia: She'd sit in the dark, twenty minutes, half an hour. Then she'd be up again. Penelope was batty. It's not good to never sleep, not once, your whole life.

Auntie Eleni: People talked. When she came over, they had to hide the good silver. You couldn't trust her.

Auntie Gigi: Who had good silver?

Yiayia: Billy's wife—Connie.

Auntie Gigi: That wasn't good silver.

Aunt Eleni: Good, solid silver.

Aunt Gigi: Silver-plated, maybe.

Yiayia: Penelope thought it was silver. That's the point.

Aunt Gigi: She was very easily satisfied.

Great-Aunt Penelope moved Ft. Lauderdale with Great-Uncle Johnny. Then—it was a Saturday—she decided to take the Caddy—a beater from the seventies, with her in the driver's seat it weighed a million pounds—to the store for an Entemann's coffee cake, and when she backed up she heard a thud-crunch. She couldn't see a thing in the mirror, but the wheels were definitely stuck. So she went forward and heard another thud-crunch. That was the thud-crunch that killed him, that second one.

Every husband hunter makes a kill after awhile.

My father wore the same grimy jeans every day. He and my brother whacked each other on the nuts and, when they got really mad, they'd punch holes in the wall.

For girls, it's important to have nice feet, slender, high-arched, for toe-shoes or kitten-heels.   For boys, it's a flush fist that matters: knuckles even, not too knobby, a broad, flat surface so they don't break their fingers when they're out smashing jaws or noses.

Every building had a super. Every super had two women: one downstairs, one upstairs. The lady upstairs—she wore silk stockings, had four screaming brats and bills to pay. A rent receipt he initialed, just an X. Red ink. Paid in full.

Black wig. Mangy stole. Gold lamé wrap. White high-heels.

Until the day he died, I thought the super was my grandfather. "He wasn't your grandfather," said Yiayia. "He couldn't even read."

When he was young, Harlan dreamed that the Philadelphia Flyers died in a bus crash and he cried the whole morning while he delivered papers.

When he spent down his liquid assets, he started borrowing money from me to pay for taxis. His new was girlfriend cabbing it all the way to Park Slope. She had a husky voice, a big ass, a pretty face, dark blonde hair, small hands. She smelled like nice lotions and all natural lavender deodorant. She didn't own sneakers.

On the Queensboro bridge, Harlan and I held hands. "Let's jump," he said. "Okay," I said. The East River is brackish, tidal. "The current is strong," I said. "It's not that strong," he said. I climbed the railing. I knew he would do it with me.

He thought we'd be fine.

Laura McCullough

Credit Rating
Laura McCullough

She has none, my friend,
        who understands the influence
        of Brecht on Benjamin
and why rhetoric matters in poetry
and also what it means to lose her credit cards,
        to live by cash,

and how to talk
        to faceless faces of the corporate entities
        that want to eat her alive,
how much to offer,
how much to hold back.   She loves Benjamin

who made up the term *auratic perception*,
        meaning ways in which a culture
        reclaims a mythology for itself,

and she undercuts the corporate gods
        by using cash only.

Each day, an angel of god
        in the voice of an Accounts Receivable Representative
        calls my friend's cell,
        a ritual.
        They think she is waiting for some kind of absolution
        for the sin of economic collapse –

the original sin we all apparently have been reborn with –

and later will field calls from accounts representatives

offering her new credit cards –
how else to regain your rating?
Remain part of the flock?

Are you still there? she asks. *Can you hear me?*

She has been reading to the ACR of the day
        from Benjamin or Hopkins,
and as usual, they've terminated the call,
        made some note about the crazy apostate
        who doesn't want to work
        on getting her credit back.
Who wouldn't do that?   They wonder.

                Is it less cruel somehow,
            when the illusion is gone,
                    to be a victim?

        More cruel to be part of the system,
                    the torturer even,
    on the stage in the theater of voracious capitalism?

                Without costumes,
            can we tell who the actors are?

        My friend takes her Blue Tooth
                out most days now,
                trolls thrift stores
        where the poor and the prosperous
            together spend their afternoons
                touching clothing
                other people
        have worn and then cast away.
        In this way, they touch each other.

76

Butterfly Leisure
Laura McCullough

Today, the woman whose mother's
        brain's image
        is flecked with pepper and rice
        grains throughout,
        will buy a small bowl
        from which she will spoon applesauce
        heavy with ginger and cinnamon
        to her mother's slack mouth.

It's a beautiful bowl, once part of a set,
        perhaps the only one left
        unsmashed in a world dangerous to china.

It's Lenox,
        which began as an art studio,
        1889, in Trenton, NJ,
and now positions itself
        as an American heritage tableware,
        and six presidents
        have commissioned "state service."

This bowl is not that,
        but it is white and vivid,
        and its gold leaf is a symbol of hope.

All for fifty cents.

Laura McCullough

And in the linens section
of the Good Will,
a huntress has passed
on the Egyptian cotton fitted sheet
the elastic of which has lost its hold.

Another woman lifts it from the floor,
knows she can repair it;
all it takes is some elastic,
her sewing machine,
and a zig zag stitch.

The rest of the set is there,
the impressions of those who've slept on it,
maybe died there, invisible,
a value added residue
implying we all lie down together.

Reclamation
Laura McCullough

At the Good Will,
        women hunt, women grieve.

There, the woman moving up and down
        the winter aisle
        touching sleeves to feel
        for cashmere vs polyester,
        mohair and wool
        vs acetates
                is glass-eyed and pale,
her mother dying of cancer,   but not today,

and she stops when her fingers find silk
        in a color she can't or won't wear,
        but draws it off the hangar
        momentarily, considering,
        before shaking her head,
        replacing it, and casting her gaze
over the tops of all the rows
        toward the linens section.

There, women are carefully and carelessly checking
        sheet sizes,
        bed throws,
        and curtains,

Laura McCullough

and a hunter is judging the quality of a set
        she's pieced together
while another stands alert nearby
        feigning disinterest
        to see what she will discard.

                It's all been discarded,
            bins and racks and shelves
                    of things
        that have been owned by someone
                    and let go.

        They are full of energy and good use,
        mostly. Waiting to be adopted.   Utilized.

            If not, they will be shipped
        to the great warehouse of used goods
    in the sky (down South, but I'm not telling where),
                the Holy Grail
            of the thrifting class.

Waiting for the Placebo Effect
Sonya Huber

My sinuses throbbed and pressed against the bones of my face like overcooked bratwurst. I pulled open the glass door of the community co-op in Columbus, Ohio. I wanted to fill my skull with brightly colored vitamin cocaine and blot out the suicide-gray Midwestern sky.

Yes, I should probably have been sitting in a doctor's office. I was an adjunct teaching writing at a local university. I was uninsured—or so I thought, but that's another story. The human resources lady didn't even mention health insurance during our two-minute tax form session that fall of 2004. No benefits packet arrived in my mailbox, so I assumed I was in the lecturer job class with all the other guns-for-hire on campus. My husband, a self-employed carpenter who I'll call Skate, fixed his swollen thumbs by drilling holes in his fingernails to let out the pus. We were do-it-yourselfers of the involuntary variety.

I spent my days swilling coffee, wincing at the onslaught of traffic and lateness and e-mails. I ate Sudafed like cinnamon red-hots. As if my South Side of Chicago accent wasn't nasal enough (Chicauuuuugo), I honked with the voice-squeezing pressure of the constantly congested. I wanted to lie down on the brownish-gray carpet and wait for a vegan staffer to drag me into the break room and heal me with camphor-and-Echinacea steam and homeopathic herbal tinctures.

Insurance was invented for ship captains in the 1660s that needed protection from the risks of the frothing, pounding sea. Once insured, these seamen could leave their wrecked vessels to founder on the rocks. Insurance was described in 1665 as "[t]he Covenant of preventing Danger... [which] added a Shadow of Law; whereby the uncertainty of the Event is usually transferred to another, with some certain Reward."

The only reward I wanted was the safety that was so near and just out of reach. It seemed to circle, to splash and taunt me, in whale-like SUVs that circled the perimeter beltway of I-270, each shiny vehicle filled with moms and kids who clearly did not worry about medical bills.

In those months I drove the snow-sludged highways toward the babysitter's, or job #1, or job #3, all freelance gigs without benefits. In a boil and fester of envy, I hated the SUVs and their drivers because each of those people was covered and therefore safe. They lived in another universe where bodies and treatments paired and came together effortlessly like ballroom dancers in layers of chiffon and satin.

I didn't want their cash. I had enough. I paid for coffees with my girlfriends, dropped an occasional $15 for a sexy shirt on sale at Urban Outfitters, and had enough pocket change for books, garage-sale clogs and thrift-store sweaters, for movies and sushi and Indian food and all the other markers of comfort for a Midwestern white girl with a few master's degrees. I had credit card balances and debt, yet I was also highly attuned to the aesthetics of a nice shoe. The skim latte cup was either half empty or half full. I didn't want cash; I wanted coverage.

In the co-op that fevered and shivery day in early 2005, I locked eyes with an Odwalla C-Monster Fruit Smoothie with 1000 percent the recommended daily allowance of vitamin C. I'm sure you have seen them: about four bucks for four mouthfuls of super-healthy puree (with profits heading straight to its parent company, Coca-Cola). Anyone who shells out cash for that scam has only herself to blame. The plastic bottle of juice stood with its cousins, shoulder to shoulder, all colors of a tropical Gauguin painting of Tahiti, in a low cooler near a tall shelf of ground yarrow root and feverfew. Cheaper juices stood in uneven rows, their dusty glass surfaces adhered with stickers, $2.00 each, offering the exact same nutrients and vitamins. The cheap juices wore labels that were slightly less pretty, the ad copy slightly more modest and realistic.

In a magazine rack at the front of the co-op, near the cash register, my safe and successful alter ego cavorted in ads for Green Investment and Eco-Tourism on the pages of *The Utne Reader.* She was a writer in Seattle or Santa Cruz, pulling her Aveda-scented hair into a ponytail, shrugging off her name-brand polar fleece, and then chugging a $3.99 Odwalla Smoothie as she piloted her new hybrid Prius on the way to a three-day yoga retreat.

I didn't want to be her.

Oh, shut up. Of course I did. I wanted to flaunt to the world, to imply with my Aveda-smelling skin and my woven fair-trade handbag that I had the embrace of Jesus and Buddha, the salvation security. I wanted to show the world the clear skin and steady gaze that comes from nights of easy sleep, organic vegetables, and lack of stress.

What was going on, in that Odwalla moment?

Ad copy ropes in an otherwise mostly sane woman: nothing unusual there. I'm not saying I'm particularly sane; I regularly spent the diaper money on spurious Glamour magazines and chocolate bars while my superego looked the other way. But this was something different, a low point for me in which specific irrational costs and benefits tipped the scales toward Odwalla. Granted, I remember that day partially because of the left-hook that would be delivered by the hippie universe before I would even finish drinking that bottle of juice. But I'll get to that.

What I see there, looking at that woman standing in front of the cooler, is healthcare fatigue. I see a woman who wanted an Odwalla bedtime story of comfort, the same safety I exuded to my baby son when I read him Snuggle Puppy for the three-trillionth time. I wanted to hear that the flannelled low-income princess could afford to make herself healthy. I clearly could not. An office visit and prescription for my sinus infection would have set me back one hundred dollars. Maybe, instead, four bucks would work.

What I needed was the curative and sustaining break from sanity. I needed three minutes, eight swallows or so, in which simple faith would grant me the illusion that my actions mattered, that my own body was under my control.

By age 33 I had yelled into a megaphone on the steps of the Ohio statehouse for universal healthcare. I had enrolled my baby son in the state program for low-income families. I had seen my picture in the newspaper and heard my voice on the radio yelling about healthcare.

By age 33, I had already been sent to collections several times for medical debt. I worried about money, which sent cortisol and other stress hormones coursing through my body, triggering the flight or flight response that proclaimed an emergency and then subtly wore me down with the effort of staying on physical alert.

By age 33, I had lived through eleven gaps in healthcare coverage. During each, I wore a groove of worry in my frontal lobe that seemed directly connected to my lymph nodes, white blood cells, and serotonin levels. I wanted to know what life would have looked like without that undercurrent of healthcare anxiety and longing. I wanted to see a version of myself, body and mind, without that skein of tension.

Most of my friends cycled in and out of the same circus. The drunks told each other that beer sterilized your throat when you had a cold. The hipsters, who had formerly spent their time bitching about how punk was not dead, developed secondary specializations in acupuncture, green algae pills, craniosacral massage, wildflower homeopathic tinctures, Reiki, Chinese medicine, and various other non-Western therapies.

I'd already done Catholicism and considered my debt to hocus pocus to have been paid. At that time in my life, I was able to finally hear the word "chakra" without throwing up, but I harbored a lingering distrust of New Age-y thinking. But I also wondered if maybe my hipster-cum-hippie friends had it right. They could take back a portion of control over their bodies. Instead of worrying, maybe I should have been romancing my adrenal and lymph systems, cooking organic stir-fry and meditating placidly while holding my sleeping infant son.

Drumming circles aside, the hippie culture of green algae pills and I had come to a sort of detente, because it seemed that receiving a squirt of herbal Rescue Remedy under the tongue took less time than whispering an extra Hail Mary. Like a doubting Catholic who goes to confession just in case, I shrugged and accepted anything that might conceivably work, including the placebo effect.

Nobody wanted to toss a barstool in rage at the cost of an ER visit or launch a punk-rock throw-down about an uninsured root canal. My women friends bitched about their boyfriends over coffee but didn't dredge up a meaty curse toward their health plans. Fixing healthcare was more hopeless and pointless than waiting for the addict to stop drugging, than getting your brother to pay you the $300 he owed you, than waiting for your favorite band to get back together. Forget it. There's always bankruptcy.

I cradled the juice in my sweaty hand, pushing a hank of long brown hair behind my ear. My glasses were probably fogged up with the transition from the gray wet cold outside to the steamy warmth of the co-op. I sniffed. I was tired, sick of carrying shredded coupons in my coat pockets. Sick of looking for the cheapest toilet paper. Sick of holding up the grocery lines with my WIC coupons while the cashier rolled her eyes and the people behind me looked me up and down. I hated the bleak cast that had settled over life itself for its potential expense. Every slip and fall, every cough, glinted with the knife-edge threat of a serious condition, a hospital visit, a debt of several thousand dollars I couldn't repay. Some weakness—a fever surge or a howl of wind outside or a sinus pang—decided it.

Fuck it. Come here, sweet immunity sports car fantasy of life-as-ad-copy. I ripped open the plastic seal and swigged the expensive juice.

The cool, sweet liquid splashed down my throat. Its thick texture felt healthy and substantial, as if it could flow to a fever-thin weak spot and fill it like vitamin spackle. I lobbed my desperation toward the icons I worshipped, as if by throwing money—$3.99 plus tax—toward a remote representative of my healthcare deity, I could curry favor.

This is the story of my torrid and twisted love affair with health insurance.

I had known its embrace. Each blissful fling unfolded with delicious expectation, wet with whispers of forevermore. I entered these brief affairs with pink hope and the best of intentions. New health insurance cards—coy valentines—always arrived in plain white envelopes. Each plastic card was like a hotel room key that unlocked its own universe of safety and security, each with its own rules. Savoring my good fortune, I browsed the provider listing and chose a fresh crew of doctors to peer into my orifices. The courting and flirting began with a bit of game playing, the waiting periods and the occasional denial of coverage for pre-existing conditions. After new love's rush of anticipation and insecurity, I made myself at home in each network, scattering the fragments of my medical history behind me like a trail of crushed candy hearts.

Take me. I'm yours. Hold me and never let me go.

I graduated from college in 1993 and leapt from the shelter of my parents' healthcare plan. The next fifteen years earned me a scattershot range of paychecks at 25 jobs. I was a receptionist many times over, a mental health counselor, a proofreader, writer, editor, reporter, assistant publisher, bookstore clerk, writing teacher, and community organizer. Eight of these gigs came with health insurance, and I latched on to those eight health plans with a desperation the employers often didn't deserve. I backed myself into gray-partitioned cubicles to get screwed by boring, dead-end, or degrading jobs, faking enthusiasm all the way for the healthcare payoff.

In between my months of insurance, I gravitated towards loser, slacker, emotionally unavailable jobs that wouldn't support my healthcare needs . I've always had a thing for the bad boys, and maybe I kept unconsciously choosing those chain-walleted, tattooed health plans that looked fine in the dim and smoky light of a fling. The second my body exhibited a need, however, these health plans turned grouchy and distant, coughing up loopholes and denials of coverage. Maybe my full-coverage, low-deductible dreamboat was still out there somewhere, bobbing above the surface of the ocean as I muttered "plenty of fish" and sorted the bottom-feeders below.

My healthcare hookup story is remarkable only in its mediocrity. I tried so hard to find The One and to discern The Rules. I hated the anonymous tryst of an emergency room visit, the feeling of a stranger's hands on my body and the knowledge that his parting words of "good luck" would be the last I'd hear from him. I wanted a prince charming—a general care practitioner, a personal care physician, a referring physician—to arrive with a fistful of referral slips. I wanted to go to an HMO where everybody knew my name.

Taking another sip, I stood in line at the register, then paid the three bucks and change. I could fake it and pretend I was in a land where $3.99 was not that big of a deal. And somehow, this juice, this brief respite from penny pinching, unknotted my shoulders and my chest. The juice tasted lovely, sweet and tangy, whirled with a slight grit. We can't always be hard, I was saying to myself, and that is also okay. Poor can't always mean the cheap juice. Crisis addressed, I swirled some juice around my teeth. I wavered in overlaps between the wooze of shame for a needless purchase and the shrug of smoothie under the bridge. Fevers would pass.

I wanted to finish the juice inside in the warm co-op before buttoning my coat and heading out, chin tucked into my collar, into the whipping wind. I crumpled the receipt into my pocket. I scanned flyers on the front bulletin board, hand-drawn ads promoting eco-friendly house cleaning and tantric pet minding.

Then I saw it: a flyer for an upcoming seminar, "Living Serenely Without Health Insurance."

Serenely. Mango-berry puree pooled beneath my tongue as my bloodstream flushed with adrenaline. I stared at the flyer, riveted. I had never entertained the vile union of these two concepts: serenity and uninsurance.

I respect people who can talk about having gratitude for their addictions, who feel blessed by their cancers, and the like. But I am not yet on that spiritual plane. I am clearly somewhere far beneath it, in an underground foxhole of healthcare. I had to force myself to take in a breath. Maybe it was the fever, but I felt attacked by that innocent poster, which seemed to be calling me out as the spiritual midget I am.

The truth was that I wanted more than anything else to live serenely without health insurance, but I wasn't sure whether that fantasy was akin to "peace within domestic violence" or "finding your pocket of calm in racial apartheid." Those pairings and strategies—strangely, profanely—are necessary to survive and yet evil to contemplate.

I wrapped my coat around me, shoved my orange knit ski cap on my head, and pushed open the glass door against the wind, gripping a half-empty bottle of juice that had lost its magic. I found my slush-encrusted car and blasted the defroster, watching the windshield wipers grate over hunks of ice on the windshield. I probably took off my glasses and cried, head down on the steering wheel, fever-flushed.

I probably fumbled with my metal-cold cell phone and called my friend Kathy, a divorced single mom living with her two kids in her parents' basement. We laughed at each other's bad days, not unkindly, because we seemed to trade the same day back and forth as we traded tips about where to apply for low-income childcare and moaned about picking up bulk quantities of peanut butter from the WIC office.

I picked up the baby from the sitter, swaddled him in layers of polar fleece and knit, wrestled him into the car seat, and drove home. I fed him and put him down for a nap. Then I went to the Internet to search for "serenity no health insurance." I wanted to see the argument and to pick it apart with my brain and my teeth, either to ravage it or to throw myself onto it for safety.

"Your search returned 0 results." Google helpfully offered to amend my query: "Did you mean to search for Serenity Now Health Insurance?"

Sure. Even better. Whatever. I clicked on the link. The screen listed Christian Web sites offering group prayer for the ill and private financial assistance for the saved. Several other search terms, a visit to Amazon, a troll through a news database all turned up nothing. This secret was so underground it was nowhere on the Web.

Fine. I would attend the workshop.

I went back to the co-op a few days later to copy down the date and time, but the poster was gone.

Health itself was no bedrock, and the body would break in time. But benefits were safety and future, lullaby and go to sleep, my feminist version of Prince Charming on a white horse, love incarnate, the thing that would make me real, would catch me when I fell and would set me back on my feet. I could not even think of my life or myself without thinking about my insurance status, and I had narrowed my sense of foundation and tomorrow to the size of a wallet-sized, white plastic card.

Contributors

Michele Carlo is a writer/performer who has lived in four of the five boroughs of NYC and remembers when a slice of pizza cost fifty cents. She has been published in M*r. Beller's Neighborhood's Lost & Found: Stories From New York, Chicken Soup For The Latino Soul* and *SMITH magazine*, and told her stories everywhere a person can tell stories in NYC—including the MOTH's GrandSlams and Mainstage, among many others. Her memoir *Fish Out Of Agua: My life on neither side of the (subway) tracks* was published by Citadel Press in August 2010. www.michelecarlo.com.

Caitlin Doyle's poetry has appeared or is forthcoming in The Atlantic Monthly, The Threepenny Review, Boston Review, Black Warrior Review, Best New Poets 2009, and others. She has held residency fellowships at a variety of artists' colonies, including the MacDowell Colony and the Ucross Foundation. She served as the Writer-In-Residence at St. Albans School in Washington, DC, and the Jack Kerouac Writer-In-Residence at the Kerouac House in Orlando, FL. Caitlin recently received the Amy Award in Poetry through Poets & Writers magazine and the Tennessee Williams Scholarship in Poetry through the Sewanee Writers Conference.

Oliver de la Paz is the author of three collections of poetry, *Names Above Houses* (SIU Press), *Furious Lullaby* (SIU Press), and *Requiem for the Orchard* (U. of Akron Press).With Stacey Lynn Brown, he co-edited *A Face to Meet the Faces: An Anthology of Contemporary Persona Poetry* (U. of Akron Press). He co-chairs the advisory board of Kundiman, a not-for-profit organization dedicated to the promotion of Asian American Poetry. A recipient of a NYFA Fellowship Award, and a GAP grant from Artists' Trust, his work has appeared in journals like *The Southern Review, Virginia Quarterly Review, North American Review, Tin House* and in anthologies such as *Asian American Poetry: The Next Generation.* He teaches at Western Washington University.

Monica A. Hand is a poet and book artist who is investigating a nomadic lifestyle as a strategy for economic, political, spiritual and artistic survival. Her manuscript, "me and Nina" received a 2010 Kinereth Gensler Award from Alice James Books and her poems have appeared in numerous publications including *Naugatuck River Review, The Sow's Ear, Drunken Boat*, and *Gathering Ground: A Reader Celebrating Cave Canem's First Decade.* She holds a MFA in Poetry and Poetry in Translation from Drew University, and is a founding member of Poets for Ayiti.

Matthea Harvey is the author of four books of poetry, including Of *Lamb* (an illustrated erasure with Amy Jean Porter), *Modern Life* and *Sad Little Breathing Machine*. She is also the author of two children's books, *The Little General and the Giant Snowflake* (illustrated by Elizabeth Zechel) and *Cecil the Pet Glacier* (illustrated by Giselle Potter).

Sonya Huber is the author of *Cover Me: A Health Insurance Memoir* and *Opa Nobody,* a hybrid work about her German socialist grandfather and her own labor activism. She has also written *The Backwards Research Guide for Writers: Using Your Life for Reflection, Connection, and Inspiration* and is working on a big unwieldy project about social class. She teaches creative writing at Fairfield University and in the Low-Residency MFA program at Ashland University.

Emmy Hunter's poetry has been published in many literary journals, including *Fence, American Poetry Review, Witness,* and *languageandculture.net.* A chapbook of her poetry and prose titled *No View of the Boat* was published by Linear Arts Press. She has been a semi-finalist for the Walt Whitman Award and the Center for Book Arts Chapbook Prize and has had residencies at Yaddo, the Virginia Center for the Arts, and the Vermont Studio Center. She teaches creative writing at Hunter College.

Leslie Jamison is the author of a novel, *The Gin Closet,* as well as stories and essays that have appeared in places like *A Public Space, The Believer, The L Magazine, Bellevue Review, Salt Hill,* and *Tin House*. She's worked as a baker, an innkeeper, a juice barista, and a medical actor. She's currently a PhD candidate in American literature at Yale University. You can find her at www.lesliejamison.com.

Rebecca Keith's poems and other writing have appeared in *Best New Poets* (2009), *The Laurel Review, The Rumpus, The Awl, BOMBlog, Dossier, Storyscape, The Millions*, and elsewhere. She holds an MFA in poetry from Sarah Lawrence College, was a semi-finalist for the 2010 "Discovery"/Boston Review poetry contest and has received honors from the *Atlantic Monthly* and *BOMB* magazine. A native of downtown New York, Rebecca is a founder, curator, and host of Mixer Reading and Music series. She also sings and plays guitar and keyboards in the Roulettes and Butchers & Bakers.

Dorianne Laux's most recent collections are *The Book of Men* and *Facts about the Moon*. A finalist for the National Book Critics Circle Award, and winner of the Oregon Book Award and The Roanoke-Chowan Award for Poetry, Laux is also author of *Awake, What We Carry*, and *Smoke* from BOA Editions. She teaches poetry in the MFA Program at North Carolina State University and is founding faculty at Pacific University's Low Residency MFA Program.

Laura McCullough has five collections of poems including, R*igger Death & Hoist Another* (013), *Panic* which won a Kinereth Gensler Award from Alice James Books, and *Speech Acts*. Her poems, essays, and interviews have appeared widely in places such as *The American Poetry Review*, The *Georgia Review, The Writer's Chronicle, Pank, Gulf Coast, Prairie Schooner,* and more. She is editor of *Between Precision and Passion: Essays on the Poetry of Stephen Dunn*, and is co-editing and anthology of essays on poetry and race with R. Dwayne Betts. She is editor of *Mead:* the Magazine of Literature and Libations.

Colleen McKee is the author of the poetry collections *My Hot Little Tomato (*which is about sex and is, in part, made of real negligee), and *A Partial List of Things I Have Done for Money* (a book whose design includes real currency). She is also co-editor of *Are We Feeling Better Yet? Women Speak About Health Care in America*. Originally from the Missouri Ozarks, Colleen now lives in Oakland, California and teaches at the Academy of Art in San Francisco. You may visit her at colleenbethmckee.blogspot.org.

Christina Olson is the author of *Before I Came Home Naked* (Spire Press, 2010). Her poetry has appeared in *Gulf Coast, Mid-American Review, Puerto del Sol*, and *Hayden's Ferry Review*, among other publications, and was selected by Gerald Stern as the winner of The *Dirty Napkin's* 2008 Poetry Prize. Her creative nonfiction appears in *Brevity, Black Warrior Review, Wake: Great Lakes Culture and Thought,* and was anthologized in

The Best Creative Nonfiction Volume 3. Originally from Buffalo, New York, she teaches at Georgia Southern University, and lives online at www.thedrevlow-olsonshow.com.

Carolyne Wright has published nine books and chapbooks of poetry, four volumes of translations from Spanish and Bengali, and a collection of essays. Her new book is *Mania Klepto: the Book of Eulene* (Turning Point, 2011). Her previous collections include *A Change of Maps* (Lost Horse Press, 2006), winner of the 2007 IPPY Bronze Award; and *Seasons of Mangoes & Brainfire* (Carnegie Mellon UP / EWU Books, 2nd edition 2005), which won the Blue Lynx Prize, Oklahoma Book Award in Poetry, and American Book Award. Wright spent a year on a Fulbright grant in Chile during the presidency of Salvador Allende; and a total of four years in Kolkata, India, and Dhaka, Bangladesh, translating the work of Bengali women poets and writers. She has written award-winning narratives about these experiences. A visiting writer at colleges and universities around the country, Wright moved back to her native Seattle in 2005, and teaches for the Northwest Institute of Literary Arts' Whidbey Writers Workshop MFA Program.

Permissions and Acknowledgements

All work printed in this anthology remains the property of the listed author unless otherwise stated on these pages.

"Minarets & Pinnacles", was reprinted with author's permission from *Pity the Bathtub Its Forced Embrace of the Human Form*, Alice James Books, 2000. ©2000, Matthea Harvey.

"Waitress", was printed with the author's permission. Copyright by Dorianne Laux.

"Spokane Reservation School Teacher: Welpinit, Washington", was reprinted with the author's permission from *Stealing the Children*, Ahsahta Press, 4th printing 1992. ©1992, Carolyne Wright.

"The Garbage Bag Wardrobe", by Colleen McKee, was printed with permission from the author. The poem previously appeared in Criminal Class Review and in the chapbook *A Partial List of Things I Have Done for Money*.

"The Broken Heart of James Agee", was printed with the author's permission. The essay previously appeared, in a slightly shorter form, in *The Believer,* January 2012. ©2012, Leslie Jamison.

CPSIA information can be obtained at www.ICGtesting.com
Printed in the USA
BVOW020915200212

283263BV00001B/7/P